Mysterious
Multiplication & D

Paul Broadbent

In a hidden cave, far away in a magical land, lives a wise wizard, called Whimstaff. Every now and again, he searches for a young apprentice, so he can pass on his magical Maths powers. And this time, Whimstaff has chosen you!

Whimstaff shares the cave with a goblin and a little, red dragon. Pointy, the goblin, is very clever. The dragon, called Miss Snufflebeam, breathes small puffs of fire. She is clumsy and often loses the wizard's magical letters and numbers.

Pointy has two greedy, pet frogs, called Mugly and Bugly, who are very lazy and spend most of their time croaking, eating and sleeping. But every so often, they amaze Pointy by helping with an exercise!

Wizard Whimstaff and his friends are very happy in their cave, solving Maths problems. Join them on a magical quest to become a fully qualified Maths wizard!

★ Contents

Letts

Terrific Times Tables

Hello, I'm Pointy, the clever goblin.
To be a wizard's assistant like me,
you need to know multiplication facts.

Use the facts you know to recall others.
Super!

	5 × 4	is	20
so	6 × 4	is 4 more	24

You'll soon get the hang of it!

Task 1 Practice makes perfect! Write the answers and colour the frog if you knew the answer instantly. Super!

a 4 × 4 = ☐   **g** 2 × 3 = ☐   **m** 4 × 5 = ☐

b 7 × 10 = ☐   **h** 5 × 2 = ☐   **n** 10 × 4 = ☐

c 3 × 3 = ☐   **i** 9 × 2 = ☐   **o** 3 × 7 = ☐

d 5 × 6 = ☐   **j** 2 × 8 = ☐   **p** 4 × 3 = ☐

e 5 × 5 = ☐   **k** 6 × 4 = ☐   **q** 10 × 6 = ☐

f 7 × 5 = ☐   **l** 2 × 10 = ☐   **r** 3 × 5 = ☐

Task 2 Wizard work so far! Now try these – write the missing numbers.

a   × 2 = 12   **e** 10 × = 30   **i** 4 × = 28

b ☆ × 3 = 18   **f** 5 × ☆ = 40   **j** ☆ × 5 = 50

c 2 × ☆ = 16   **g** ☆ × 4 = 36   **k** ☆ × 4 = 32

d 2 × ☆ = 14   **h** ☆ × 3 = 24   **l** 5 × ☆ = 45

Task 3 Continue these shooting star patterns. It's easy when you know how!

a 2 4 6

b 100 90 80

c 5 10 15

d 3 6 9

e 40 36 32

f 20 18 16

Sorcerer's Skill Check

Wizard Whimstaff makes magical number puzzles for clever goblins like me. As you have worked so hard, you can complete this one!

Across
a 3 × 9
b 2 × 8
c 10 × 4
d 4 × 8
e 5 × 3
g 5 × 5
h 7 × 4
i 2 × 10
j 7 × 2
k 2 × 2
l 3 × 3

Down
a 3 × 8
b 2 × 6
c 5 × 9
d 7 × 5
e 6 × 3
f 10 × 8
g 7 × 3
h 4 × 6
i 5 × 4

a		b		c	
	d		e		f
g		h		i	
j			k		l

Well completed, my apprentice! Add a gold star to your certificate.

Tricky Times Tables

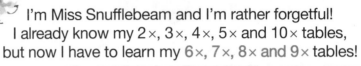

I'm Miss Snufflebeam and I'm rather forgetful!
I already know my 2×, 3×, 4×, 5× and 10× tables,
but now I have to learn my 6×, 7×, 8× and 9× tables!

Perhaps this will help me.

3 × 8 gives the same answer as 8 × 3.   3 × 8 = 24
                                            8 × 3 = 24

Cabradababa! Knowing 2×, 3×, 4×, 5× and
10× tables means that you know many of the
facts for your 6×, 7×, 8× and 9× tables!

Task 1 Rabracadada! Are you ready? Write the answers and colour the quill if you knew the answer instantly.

a 2 × 9 = ☐   **b** 4 × 6 = ☐   **c** 3 × 7 = ☐

d 9 × 5 = ☐   **e** 6 × 10 = ☐

f 8 × 3 = ☐   **g** 7 × 2 = ☐   **h** 6 × 5 = ☐

Task 2 Oh dear! These are much harder. Can you help by writing in the answer for each of these?

a 8 × 8 = ☐   **b** 7 × 9 = ☐   **c** 7 × 6 = ☐   **d** 9 × 9 = ☐

e 6 × 9 = ☐   **f** 8 × 7 = ☐   **g** 6 × 6 = ☐   **h** 8 × 6 = ☐

Task 3 What a mess! I've splodged ink everywhere. Can you write the missing numbers on the splodges?

a ☐ × 8 = 16   **d** 7 × ☐ = 35   **g** ☐ × 9 = 27   **j** 6 × ☐ = 60

b 6 × ☐ = 48   **e** ☐ × 9 = 81   **h** 8 × ☐ = 56   **k** ☐ × 7 = 42

c 9 × ☐ = 72   **f** ☐ × 7 = 28   **i** ☐ × 9 = 18   **l** 6 × ☐ = 30

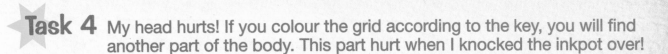

★ Task 4 My head hurts! If you colour the grid according to the key, you will find another part of the body. This part hurt when I knocked the inkpot over!

64	16	8	7	28	14	36	54	18
46	32	20	14	26	63	60	25	22
9	40	15	70	34	21	12	36	6
38	80	44	63	20	49	54	15	53
47	88	27	28	35	70	30	60	18

Remember the numbers in a times table are called multiples.
6 × 3 is 18.
18 is a multiple of 3 and 6.

Multiples of 6 – green

Multiples of 7 – red

Multiples of 8 – blue

Sorcerer's Skill Check

Dabracababra! My magic won't work! These cauldrons are supposed to multiply numbers. Those two lazy frogs – Mugly and Bugly – won't help, so can you write the numbers that should come out of each cauldron?

a 8
b 4
c 6
d 5
e 9

f 9
g 6
h 8
i 7
j 3

IN ×9 OUT

IN ×7 OUT

Slurp … give yourself a gold star! Is it time for a snooze yet?

5

Dazzling Doubling

Hello, young apprentice, I'm Wizard Whimstaff and I'm here to help you become a maths wizard! Hey Presto! Here's a dazzling doubling method to make multiplying large numbers easy!

If you know that   6 × 2 is 12   then …
Allakazan!   60 × 2 = 120

To work out double 63, do it in two stages:

double 60   is 120
double 3   is   6
so, double 63   = 120 + 6 = 126.

Now have a go at the exercises.

Task 1
These doubles will be no trouble! Write the double for each of these and colour the spoon if you knew the answer instantly.

a 45 × 2 =

b 23 × 2 =

c 90 × 2 =

d 15 × 2 =

e 52 × 2 =

f 18 × 2 =

g 24 × 2 =

h 48 × 2 =

Task 2
These are a bit harder – just do the best you can on the task, my apprentice.

a	71 × 2 =	d	26 × 2 =	g	64 × 2 =	j	39 × 2 =
b	67 × 2 =	e	85 × 2 =	h	99 × 2 =	k	57 × 2 =
c	96 × 2 =	f	38 × 2 =	i	86 × 2 =	l	78 × 2 =

Task 3
For the spells I'm cooking, I need to double. Read the questions carefully and write each answer.

a What is double 28?

b What is 75 doubled?

c Double 66.

d What is twice 59?

e What is 34 multiplied by 2?

f Multiply 47 by 2.

Task 4
Task 4 I have used half the potions and powders from each of these pots. Write the amount that was in each pot when it was full.

a 240 g

full _____ g

b 160 ml

full _____ ml

c 93 ml

full _____ ml

d 550 ml

full _____ ml

e 700 g

full _____ g

f 320 g

full _____ g

g 108 g

full _____ g

h 215 ml

full _____ ml

i 142 g

full _____ g

j 337 ml

full _____ ml

Sorcerer's Skill Check

These are my empty magic pattern potion jars. Miss Snufflebeam has started each row, filling them with number patterns. Can you complete these by doubling numbers for her?

a 10 20

b 9 18

c 13 26

d 6 12

Cabradababa! Another gold star! You'll be as brainy as Wizard Whimstaff soon!

7

Marvellous Multiples

We're Mugly and Bugly. Burp! Multiplying by 10 is what we want to do to our dinner!

Croak … when multiplying a number by 10, each digit of the number moves one place to the left. The empty spaces are filled with zeros.

$20 \times 10 = 200$

H	T	U		
	2	0	×	10
2	0	0		

When multiplying by 100, each digit moves two places to the left. The empty spaces are filled with zeros.

$60 \times 100 = 6000$

Th	H	T	U		
		6	0	×	100
6	0	0	0		

20×30?
$20 \times 3 = 60$
$60 \times 10 = 600$
$20 \times 30 = 600$

★ Task 1 After all that explaining, we'll let you complete these cobweb number puzzles – we're off for a snooze! Multiply each number by the middle number and write the answers around the outside.

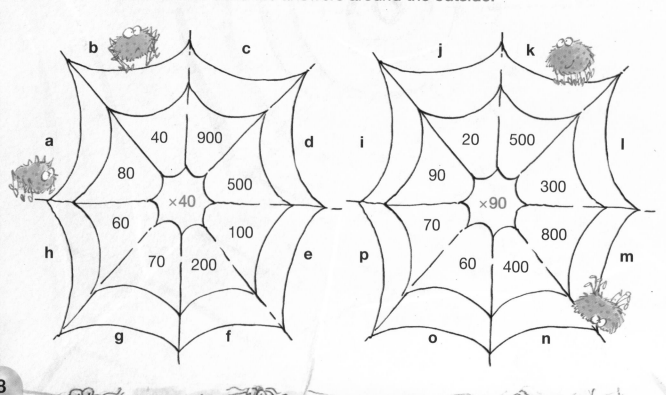

8

Task 2

Croak … write the answers for these. Careful, if you get too clever we'll have to call you Pointy.

> Remember, when multiplying by 100, the digits move **two** places to the left.

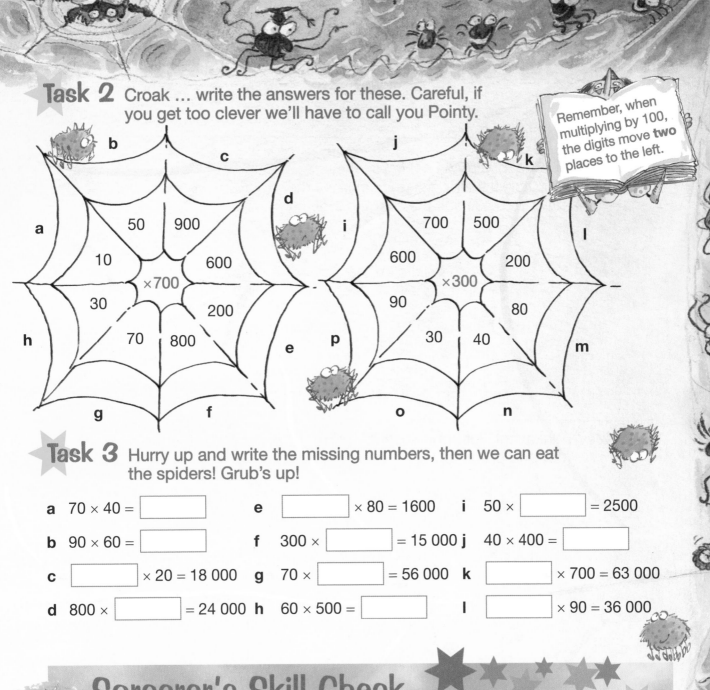

Task 3

Hurry up and write the missing numbers, then we can eat the spiders! Grub's up!

a $70 \times 40 = \boxed{}$

b $90 \times 60 = \boxed{}$

c $\boxed{} \times 20 = 18\,000$

d $800 \times \boxed{} = 24\,000$

e $\boxed{} \times 80 = 1600$

f $300 \times \boxed{} = 15\,000$

g $70 \times \boxed{} = 56\,000$

h $60 \times 500 = \boxed{}$

i $50 \times \boxed{} = 2500$

j $40 \times 400 = \boxed{}$

k $\boxed{} \times 700 = 63\,000$

l $\boxed{} \times 90 = 36\,000$

Sorcerer's Skill Check

Slurp! Can you complete these number grids?

a

×	80	40	60
70			
500			
800			
300			

b

×	300	700	600
20			
90			
40			
60			

Super! You can now add your gold star to your certificate.

Magical Mental Methods

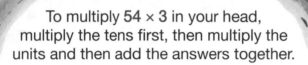

To multiply 54 × 3 in your head, multiply the tens first, then multiply the units and then add the answers together.

Hey Presto!

$50 × 3 = 150$
$4 × 3 = 12$

so, $54 × 3 = 150 + 12 = 162$

Task 1 Allakazan! Put your wizard's thinking hat on and write the answers for each of these.

a	60 × 4 =	d	30 × 7 =	g	80 × 5 =	j	40 × 9 =
	2 × 4 =		6 × 7 =		5 × 5 =		3 × 9 =
	62 × 4 =		36 × 7 =		85 × 5 =		43 × 9 =
b	20 × 8 =	e	50 × 6 =	h	90 × 3 =	k	70 × 4 =
	6 × 8 =		5 × 6 =		7 × 3 =		4 × 4 =
	26 × 8 =		55 × 6 =		97 × 3 =		74 × 4 =
c	80 × 7 =	f	90 × 6 =	i	60 × 3 =	l	40 × 8 =
	8 × 7 =		3 × 6 =		5 × 3 =		9 × 8 =
	88 × 7 =		93 × 6 =		65 × 3 =		49 × 8 =

Task 2 Abracadabra! Work these out in your head and then write the answers. Don't worry if it seems hard at first.

a	27 × 5 =	b	42 × 8 =	c	35 × 4 =
d	64 × 9 =	e	78 × 3 =	f	56 × 7 =

Task 3

These are the things I want to buy from the Sorcerer's Superstore. Can you write the total cost for each of these?

a 3 wizard's wands cost £_____

b 5 wizard's hats cost £_____

c 7 wizard's cloaks cost £_____

d 4 wizard's broomsticks cost £_____

e 9 wizard's wands cost £_____

f 8 wizard's hats cost £_____

g 9 wizard's cloaks cost £_____

h 6 wizard's broomsticks cost £_____

£98

£45

£72

£26

Sorcerer's Skill Check

Hey Presto! To perform this special spell, write the answers and then cast a circle around the matching numbers written in words in this search puzzle.

a $4 \times 15 =$ [ ]

b $27 \times 3 =$ [ ]

c $18 \times 5 =$ [ ]

d $16 \times 6 =$ [ ]

e $20 \times 4 =$ [ ]

f $23 \times 3 =$ [ ]

E	V	I	F	Y	T	R	O	F
N	I	N	E	T	Y	S	I	X
I	D	G	W	U	L	Z	Y	Y
N	Y	T	H	G	I	E	T	T
Y	F	I	F	T	Y	P	E	R
T	S	I	X	T	Y	B	N	O
X	K	J	Z	N	M	O	I	F
I	F	I	F	T	Y	O	N	E
S	E	V	E	N	T	Y	C	E

g $25 \times 2 =$ [ ]

h $15 \times 3 =$ [ ]

i $20 \times 2 =$ [ ]

j $17 \times 3 =$ [ ]

k $35 \times 2 =$ [ ]

Slurp! You show signs of being as good as Pointy! Give yourself a gold star.

Wacky Written Methods

When multiplying large numbers for Wizard Whimstaff, I find that it's sometimes easier to use a wacky written method.

Look at these two written methods of multiplying 273×8.

×	2 0 0	+	7 0	+	3		
8	1 6 0 0	+	5 6 0	+	2 4	=	2 1 8 4

	2	7	3	
×			8	
	1 6	0	0	200×8
	5	6	0	70×8
+		2	4	3×8
	2 1	8	4	

Task 1   Now you have a try! Complete these by using the first wacky written method.

a 463×3

×	4 0 0	+	6 0	+	3		
3		+		+		=	

b 839×6

×	8 0 0	+	3 0	+	9		
6		+		+		=	

c 752×9

×	7 0 0	+	5 0	+	2		
9		+		+		=	

d 694×7

×	6 0 0	+	9 0	+	4		
7		+		+		=	

Task 2   Super! Now try the other wacky written method to find the answers for these.

a 347×5

	3	4	7	
×			5	
				300×5
				40×5
+				7×5

b 925×8

	9	2	5	
×			8	
				900×8
				20×8
+				5×8

c 578×4

	5	7	8	
×			4	
				500×4
				70×4
+				8×4

Task 3 It's easy when you know how! Choose the method you found easiest and use it to find the answers to each of these.

a 815 × 6 =

c 396 × 5 =

b 274 × 8 =

d 779 × 9 =

Working out area:

Sorcerer's Skill Check

Can you prove you're a maths whizz by completing these multiplications?

a 570 × 8

×	5	0	0	+	7	0	+	0			
8				+			+		=		

b 962 × 5

×	9	0	0	+	6	0	+	2		
5				+			+		=	

c 409 × 7

		4	0	9
×				7
+				

d 836 × 4

		8	3	6
×				4
+				

Oh, you have done well! Rabracadada! Another gold star!

Apprentice Wizard Challenge 1

Challenge 1 Complete this number puzzle.

Across

a 3 × 7
c 4 × 3
e 4 × 9
h 10 × 4
i 5 × 9
k 3 × 9
m 2 × 8
o 3 × 3
p 5 × 5

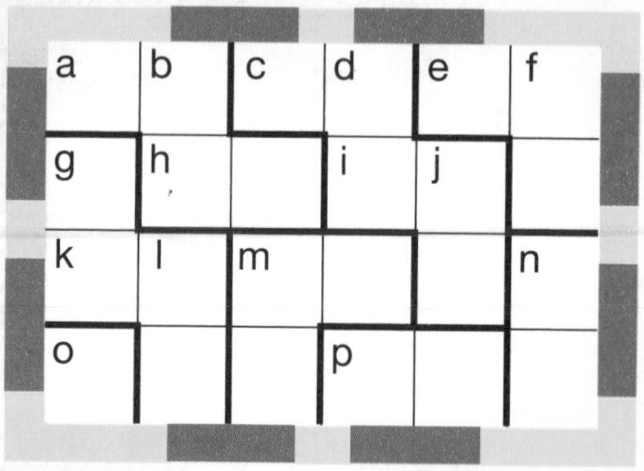
a b c d e f
g h i j
k l m n
o p

Down

b 2 × 7
d 4 × 6
f 10 × 6
g 4 × 8
j 5 × 10
l 10 × 7
m 2 × 9
n 3 × 8

Challenge 2 Answer these.

a 6 × 7 = ___
b 6 × 9 = ___
c 7 × 8 = ___
d 7 × 7 = ___
e 9 × 8 = ___
f 8 × 8 = ___
g 9 × 9 = ___
h 8 × 6 = ___
i 6 × 6 = ___
j 4 × 7 = ___
k 5 × 8 = ___
l 7 × 5 = ___
m 4 × 7 = ___
n 6 × 3 = ___
o 7 × 9 = ___
p 9 × 4 = ___

Challenge 3 Complete these shooting star patterns by doubling.

a

2
4

b

7
14

c

45
90

Challenge 4 Complete these number grids.

a

×	30	90	50
300			
800			
600			

b

×	200	400	700
10			
70			
80			

Challenge 5 Write the total cost for each of these.

a £18

7 wands cost:

£ _____

b £27

5 broomsticks cost:

£ _____

c £44

6 wizard's hats cost:

£ _____

d £65

9 cauldrons cost:

£ _____

Challenge 6 Choose a written method to find the answer to each of these.

a $314 \times 4 =$ ☐   **b** $628 \times 8 =$ ☐   **c** $590 \times 3 =$ ☐   **d** $775 \times 9 =$ ☐

Working out area:

What a super effort! Give yourself another gold star!

Devilish Division Facts

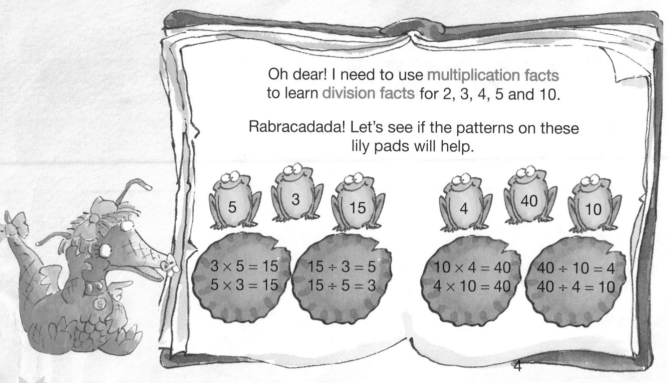

Oh dear! I need to use multiplication facts to learn division facts for 2, 3, 4, 5 and 10.

Rabracadada! Let's see if the patterns on these lily pads will help.

$3 \times 5 = 15$
$5 \times 3 = 15$

$15 \div 3 = 5$
$15 \div 5 = 3$

$10 \times 4 = 40$
$4 \times 10 = 40$

$40 \div 10 = 4$
$40 \div 4 = 10$

Task 1   My head hurts – can you help with these? Write the facts for these trios.

a

☐ × ☐ = ☐   ☐ ÷ ☐ = ☐
☐ × ☐ = ☐   ☐ ÷ ☐ = ☐

d
☐ × ☐ = ☐   ☐ ÷ ☐ = ☐
☐ × ☐ = ☐   ☐ ÷ ☐ = ☐

b

☐ × ☐ = ☐   ☐ ÷ ☐ = ☐
☐ × ☐ = ☐   ☐ ÷ ☐ = ☐

e

☐ × ☐ = ☐   ☐ ÷ ☐ = ☐
☐ × ☐ = ☐   ☐ ÷ ☐ = ☐

c

☐ × ☐ = ☐   ☐ ÷ ☐ = ☐
☐ × ☐ = ☐   ☐ ÷ ☐ = ☐

f

☐ × ☐ = ☐   ☐ ÷ ☐ = ☐
☐ × ☐ = ☐   ☐ ÷ ☐ = ☐

Task 2 I'm confused! Can you write the answers for these? Tick the toad if you knew the answer instantly.

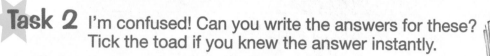

Remember to use your multiplication facts to help with these divisions.

a $10 \div 5 =$ ☐

b $8 \div 2 =$ ☐

c $28 \div 4 =$ ☐

d $36 \div 4 =$ ☐

e $30 \div 5 =$ ☐

f $70 \div 10 =$ ☐

g $12 \div 3 =$ ☐

h $30 \div 10 =$ ☐

i $45 \div 5 =$ ☐

j $100 \div 10 =$ ☐

k $60 \div 10 =$ ☐

l $27 \div 3 =$ ☐

m $6 \div 3 =$ ☐

n $16 \div 2 =$ ☐

o $4 \div 2 =$ ☐

p $24 \div 4 =$ ☐

Sorcerer's Skill Check

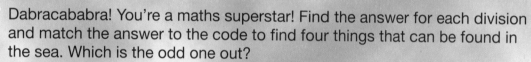

Dabracababra! You're a maths superstar! Find the answer for each division and match the answer to the code to find four things that can be found in the sea. Which is the odd one out?

a $90 \div 10 =$ ☐ ☐

   $16 \div 4 =$ ☐ ☐

   $18 \div 3 =$ ☐ ☐

   $20 \div 4 =$ ☐ ☐

   $24 \div 3 =$ ☐ ☐

b $14 \div 2 =$ ☐ ☐

   $40 \div 5 =$ ☐ ☐

   $24 \div 4 =$ ☐ ☐

   $50 \div 10 =$ ☐ ☐

Code:

3	4	5	6	7	8	9
t	h	l	a	s	e	w

c $35 \div 5 =$ ☐ ☐

   $12 \div 2 =$ ☐ ☐

   $25 \div 5 =$ ☐ ☐

   $9 \div 3 =$ ☐ ☐

d $32 \div 4 =$ ☐ ☐

   $80 \div 10 =$ ☐ ☐

   $15 \div 3 =$ ☐ ☐

The odd one out

is _____.

Well completed, my apprentice! Add a gold star to your certificate.

Dastardly Division

Slurp … use multiplication facts to learn division facts 6, 7, 8 and 9.

$42 \div 7 = ?$ $42 \div 6 = ?$

Burp … How many sevens in 42?
How many sixes in 42?

$6 \times 7 = 42$
There are 6 sevens in 42.

$7 \times 6 = 42$
Croak … There are 7 sixes in 42.

Task 1 Have a go at this exercise – if you can spare the time. Is it time for a snooze yet?

a $40 \div 8 =$ d $28 \div 7 =$ g $36 \div 6 =$ j $27 \div 9 =$

b $14 \div 7 =$ e $90 \div 9 =$ h $24 \div 8 =$ k $49 \div 7 =$

c $54 \div 6 =$ f $18 \div 9 =$ i $64 \div 8 =$ l $63 \div 9 =$

Task 2 Brain cell alert! Some of these numbers have gone missing. Can you write the missing numbers?

a $56 \div = 8$ d $18 \div 6 =$ g $81 \div = 9$ j $72 \div = 8$

b $48 \div 8 =$ e $30 \div = 6$ h $42 \div = 7$ k $24 \div 6 =$

c $ \times 3 = 24$ f $6 \times = 54$ i $ \times 7 = 49$ l $8 \times = 40$

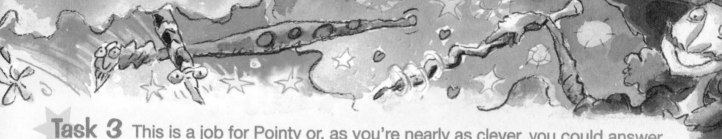

Task 3
This is a job for Pointy or, as you're nearly as clever, you could answer these word problems.

a What is 56 shared equally by 7? ☐

b How many sevens are there in 21? ☐

c How many weeks are there in 35 days? ☐

d Divide 36 by 6. ☐

e What is half of 14? ☐

f Divide 8 into 16. ☐

Task 4
Flies – grub's up! We're off for dinner – answer these while we're gone.

a 36 flies were shared equally between 9 frogs. How many flies did each frog get?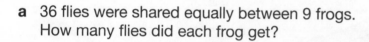

b Pointy spent 42p on 6 balloons. How much did one balloon cost? p

c A wand 72 cm long is cut into 8 equal pieces. How long is each piece of wand? cm

d An elf egg box holds 6 eggs. How many boxes can be filled with 48 eggs?

e Miss Snufflebeam shares 45 cloud cakes equally between 9 pixies. How many cloud cakes does she give each pixie? ☐

Sorcerer's Skill Check

Slurp! We've dropped a bag of stars. Can you fill in the missing numbers?

a ☆ $\div 7 = 5$

b $28 \div$ ☆ $= 7$

c $6 \times$ ☆ $= 18$

d $81 \div$ ☆ $= 9$

e ☆ $\div 8 = 10$

f ☆ $\times 8 = 64$

g ☆ $\div 6 = 2$

h ☆ $\times 9 = 36$

i $9 \times$ ☆ $= 63$

Another gold star! Cabradababa! You have done well.

19

Hazardous Halving

Knowing doubles can help with halving! Super!

Double 34 is 68.   Double 75 is 150.
Half of 68 is 34.   Half of 150 is 75.

To halve larger numbers, halve the hundreds, halve the tens and then halve the units.

To help Wizard Whimstaff, I need to find half of 476.

Half of 400   is 200.
Half of 70   is 35.
Half of 6   is 3.

So, half of 476   is 238.

You'll soon get the hang of it!

Task 1 Now you have a try! Halve each of these numbers.

a 48 ÷ 2 =   b 62 ÷ 2 =   c 90 ÷ 2 =   d 72 ÷ 2 =

e 56 ÷ 2 =   f 500 ÷ 2 =   g 300 ÷ 2 =   h 120 ÷ 2 =

Task 2 Here are some more numbers for you to halve. Practice makes perfect!

a 108 ÷ 2 =   b 230 ÷ 2 =   c 168 ÷ 2 =   d 450 ÷ 2 =

e 296 ÷ 2 =   f 314 ÷ 2 =   g 742 ÷ 2 =   h 336 ÷ 2 =

Task 3 These are a bit harder, but not half as hard as you think!

a 1000 ÷ 2 =   b 2400 ÷ 2 =   c 5200 ÷ 2 =

d 8400 ÷ 2 =   e 7600 ÷ 2 =   f 3600 ÷ 2 =

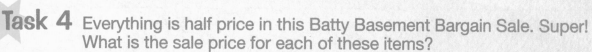

Task 4

Everything is half price in this Batty Basement Bargain Sale. Super! What is the sale price for each of these items?

a

Was: £28

Now: £_____

b

Was: £32

Now: £_____

c

Was: £15

Now: £_____

d

Was: £116

Now: £_____

e

Was: £176

Now: £_____

f

Was: £249

Now: £_____

Sorcerer's Skill Check

Work your magic to complete these number chains by halving.

a	800	400					
b	5600	2800					
c	768	384					
d	1280	640					

Slurp! Give yourself a gold star! Careful – if you get too clever, we might have to call you Pointy!

Dreamy Dividing

Oh dear, I'll never understand dividing by 10 and 100.

Oh, I remember, when dividing a number **by 10**, each digit of the number moves **one place** to the right. Rabracadada!

Th	H	T	U
6	4	0	0	÷ 10
	6	4	0	

When dividing **by 100** they move **two places** to the right. Dabracababra!

Th	H	T	U
2	7	0	0	÷ 100
		2	7	

★ Task 1 Can you work these out in your head? My head hurts!

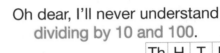

a 7100 ÷ 10 =

b 1200 ÷ 10 =

c 3000 ÷ 10 =

d 9700 ÷ 10 =

e 1000 ÷ 10 =

f 5500 ÷ 10 =

g 800 ÷ 10 =

h 260 ÷ 10 =

★ Task 2 Oh no, these are even harder! Can you write the answers?

a 2400 ÷ 100 = ⬚

b 6300 ÷ 100 = ⬚

c 4000 ÷ 100 = ⬚

d 700 ÷ 100 = ⬚

e 7600 ÷ 100 = ⬚

f 9900 ÷ 100 = ⬚

g 1000 ÷ 100 = ⬚

h 300 ÷ 100 = ⬚

Remember – when dividing by 100, the digits move two places to the right.

Task 3 This looks fun! Draw a line from each hat to the bat with the correct answer. More than one hat might match a bat.

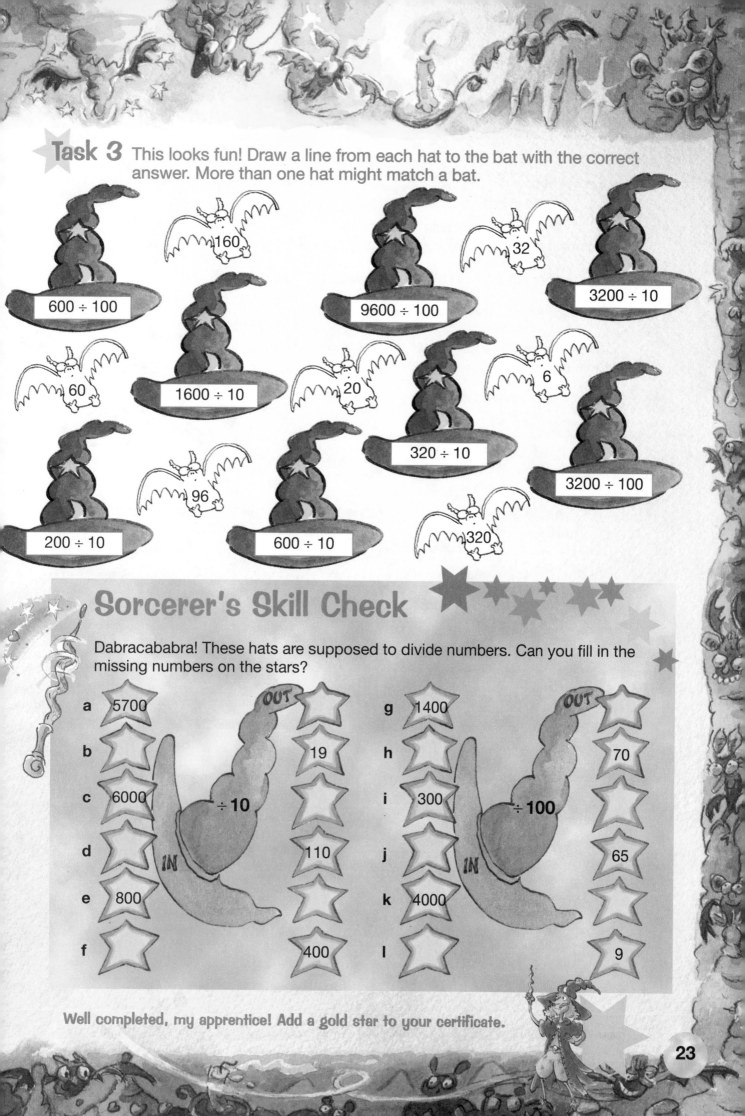

160

600 ÷ 100

32

9600 ÷ 100

3200 ÷ 10

60

1600 ÷ 10

20

6

320 ÷ 10

96

200 ÷ 10

600 ÷ 10

320

3200 ÷ 100

Sorcerer's Skill Check

Dabracababra! These hats are supposed to divide numbers. Can you fill in the missing numbers on the stars?

OUT ÷ 10 IN

a 5700
b
c 6000
d
e 800
f

19

110

400

OUT ÷ 100 IN

g 1400
h
i 300
j
k 4000
l

70

65

9

Well completed, my apprentice! Add a gold star to your certificate.

23

Revolting Remainders

Croak … sometimes a number cannot be divided exactly by another number.

The number left over is called the remainder.

Burp! Nothing's left over when we're eating!

Brain cell alert! The remainder can be shown as a whole number or as a decimal.

$$34 \div 4 = 8 \text{ r } 2$$
$$\text{or} = 8.5$$

Task 1 This is a job for Pointy! Write each answer with a remainder as a whole number.

a $19 \div 2 =$ r

b $27 \div 6 =$ r

c $38 \div 5 =$ r

d $46 \div 4 =$ r

e $45 \div 6 =$ r

f $49 \div 5 =$ r

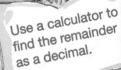

Use a calculator to find the remainder as a decimal.

Task 2 Is it time for a snooze yet? We'll let you write these remainders as decimals.

a $35 \div 2 =$.

b $50 \div 8 =$.

c $30 \div 4 =$.

d $16 \div 5 =$.

e $21 \div 5 =$.

f $68 \div 8 =$.

g $86 \div 8 =$.

h $22 \div 4 =$.

Task 3 Slurp! Work out the cost for one of each of these items whilst we have a snack!

a 2 for £3.00

Cost of 1 = £_____

b 10 for £6.00

Cost of 1 = _____p

c 5 for £4.00

Cost of 1 = _____p

d 8 for £10.00

Cost of 1 = £_____

e 5 for £12

Cost of 1 = £_____

f 4 for £7.00

Cost of 1 = £_____

g 6 for £9.00

Cost of 1 = £_____

h 5 for £16.00

Cost of 1 = £_____

Sorcerer's Skill Check

We're worn out now. Work out how many will be left over when … zzzz …

a 20 eggs are shared equally between 3 egg boxes.

b 7 goblins share 40 bearded biscuits equally.

c 28 elves are divided into 5 equal teams.

d 37 wands are tied into bunches of 6.

e 52 bats are put in equal numbers into 9 caves.

f 4 giants share 45 trolls equally.

You can now add your gold star to your certificate, young apprentice! Super!

Written Wizardry

When dividing large numbers, it is easier to use a wizard written method.

```
          4  3  r  1
   8 │ 3  4  5
     − 3  2  0      (8 × 4)
          2  5
     −    2  4      (8 × 3)
          r  1
```

So the answer to 345 ÷ 8 is 43 r 1.

Task 1 Hey presto! Work out the answers to these. Just do the best you can on the task, my apprentice.

a
```
              r
  9 │ 2  9  4
  −

  −
        r
```

b
```
              r
  4 │ 3  1  3
  −

  −
        r
```

c
```
              r
  7 │ 5  0  8
  −

  −
        r
```

d
```
              r
  6 │ 1  7  6
  −

  −
        r
```

e
```
              r
  5 │ 4  2  9
  −

  −
        r
```

f
```
              r
  3 │ 2  6  2
  −

  −
        r
```

g
```
              r
  8 │ 6  5  5
  −

  −
        r
```

h
```
              r
  4 │ 3  4  7
  −

  −
        r
```

i
```
              r
  9 │ 4  0  6
  −

  −
        r
```

j
```
              r
  5 │ 3  7  2
  −

  −
        r
```

⭐ **Task 2** You have worked well! Now have a go at this exercise. Write the missing numbers.

a

		8	6	r	1
2	1	7			
−					
−					
		r			

b

		4	3	r	4
7		0	5		
−					
−					
		r			

c

		7	4	r	1
4	2		7		
−					
−					
		r			

d

		9	8	r	6
9	8		8		
−					
−					
		r			

e

		8	4	r	7
8		7	9		
−					
−					
		r			

f

		8	5	r	1
5	4	2			
−					
−					
		r			

Sorcerer's Skill Check

You are getting as clever as my goblin assistant, Pointy! Complete this final task by working out the answers to these. Allakazan!

a

				r	
6	4	1	1		
−					
−					
			r		

b

				r	
3	1	5	8		
−					
−					
			r		

c

				r	
8	2	9	8		
−					
−					
			r		

d

				r	
7	3	7	0		
−					
−					
			r		

e

				r	
4	2	1	5		
−					
−					
			r		

Dabracababra! Oh dear, I got that all wrong, but you deserve another gold star!

Apprentice Wizard Challenge 2

Challenge 1 Have a go at answering these word problems.

a Miss Snufflebeam bought a pack of 3 cobweb cakes for 27p. How much did one cake cost? ⬚ p

b 32 pixies are put into 4 equal teams. How many pixies will there be in each team? ⬚

c A piece of spider's silk is 70 cm long. How many 10 cm strips can be cut out? ⬚

d Divide 12 by 4. ⬚

e How many fives are there in 30? ⬚

f Share 100 between 10. ⬚

g What is half of 12 kg? ⬚ kg

Challenge 2 Wave your magic wand and answer these.

a $24 \div 6 =$ ⬚   d $90 \div 9 =$ ⬚   g $16 \div 8 =$ ⬚

b $45 \div 9 =$ ⬚   e $21 \div 7 =$ ⬚   h $54 \div 9 =$ ⬚

c $56 \div 7 =$ ⬚   f $40 \div 8 =$ ⬚   i $48 \div 6 =$ ⬚

Challenge 3 There is a half-price sale in the pixie pet shop. Write the sale price for each of these.

a
was £14
Sale price
£_____

d
was £34
Sale price
£_____

b
was £26
Sale price
£_____

e
was £48
Sale price
£_____

c

was £50
Sale price
£_____

f

was £62
Sale price
£_____

Challenge 4

Write the missing numbers on the puffs of smoke as they go in and out of the jars.

a 300

b   670

c 8500

d   32

e 40

IN ÷10 OUT

f 600

g   8

h 7200

i   59

j 100

IN ÷100 OUT

Challenge 5

Write each answer with the remainder as a whole number and as a decimal.

a $13 \div 2 =$ ⬡ r ⬡
⬡ . ⬡

d $39 \div 6 =$ ⬡ r ⬡
⬡ . ⬡

g $43 \div 2 =$ ⬡ r ⬡
⬡ . ⬡

b $60 \div 8 =$ ⬡ r ⬡
⬡ . ⬡

e $15 \div 6 =$ ⬡ r ⬡
⬡ . ⬡

h $19 \div 5 =$ ⬡ r ⬡
⬡ . ⬡

c $21 \div 4 =$ ⬡ r ⬡
⬡ . ⬡

f $34 \div 8 =$ ⬡ r ⬡
⬡ . ⬡

i $52 \div 5 =$ ⬡ r ⬡
⬡ . ⬡

Challenge 6

Work out the answers.

a

				r	
3	7	0	3		
−					
−					
				r	

b

				r	
7	4	2	8		
−					
−					
				r	

c

				r	
9	5	1	1		
−					
−					
				r	

d

				r	
4	6	9	3		
−					
−					
				r	

Croak! Your hard work has made us hungry! We'll have a snack while you have a gold star!

Answers

Pages 2–3

Task 1
a	16	j	16
b	70	k	24
c	9	l	20
d	30	m	20
e	25	n	40
f	35	o	21
g	6	p	12
h	10	q	60
i	18	r	15

Task 2
a	6	g	9
b	6	h	8
c	8	i	7
d	7	j	10
e	3	k	8
f	8	l	9

Task 3
a	8 10 12 14 16 18 20
b	70 60 50 40 30 20 10
c	20 25 30 35 40 45 50
d	12 15 18 21 24 27 30
e	28 24 20 16 12 8 4
f	14 12 10 8 6 4 2

Sorcerer's Skill Check

Across		**Down**	
a	27	a	24
b	16	b	12
c	40	c	45
d	32	d	35
e	15	e	18
g	25	f	80
h	28	g	21
i	20	h	24
j	14	i	20
k	4		
l	9		

Pages 4–5

Task 1
a	18	e	60
b	24	f	24
c	21	g	14
d	45	h	30

Task 2
a	64	e	54
b	63	f	56
c	42	g	36
d	81	h	48

Task 3
a	2	g	3
b	8	h	7
c	8	i	2
d	5	j	10
e	9	k	6
f	4	l	5

Task 4 TOE

Sorcerer's Skill Check
a	72	f	63
b	36	g	42
c	54	h	56
d	45	i	49
e	81	j	21

Pages 6–7

Task 1
a	90	e	104
b	46	f	36
c	180	g	48
d	30	h	96

Task 2
a	142	g	128
b	134	h	198
c	192	i	172
d	52	j	78
e	170	k	114
f	76	l	156

Task 3
a	56	d	118
b	150	e	68
c	132	f	94

Task 4
a	480 g	f	640 g
b	320 ml	g	216 g
c	186 ml	h	430 ml
d	1100 ml	i	284 g
e	1400 g	j	674 ml

Sorcerer's Skill Check
a	40 80 160 320 640
b	36 72 144 288 576
c	52 104 208 416 832
d	24 48 96 192 384

Pages 8–9

Task 1
a	3200	i	8100
b	1600	j	1800
c	36 000	k	45 000
d	20 000	l	27 000
e	4000	m	72 000
f	8000	n	36 000
g	2800	o	5400
h	2400	p	6300

Task 2
a	7000	i	180 000
b	35 000	j	210 000
c	630 000	k	150 000
d	420 000	l	60 000
e	140 000	m	24 000
f	560 000	n	12 000
g	49 000	o	9000
h	21 000	p	27 000

Task 3
a	2800	g	800
b	5400	h	30 000
c	900	i	50
d	30	j	16 000
e	20	k	90
f	50	l	400

Sorcerer's Skill Check
a	5600	2800	4200
	40 000	20 000	30 000
	64 000	32 000	48 000
	24 000	12 000	18 000
b	6000	14 000	12 000
	27 000	63 000	54 000
	12 000	28 000	24 000
	18 000	42 000	36 000

Pages 10–11

Task 1
a	240	g	400
	8		25
	248		425
b	160	h	270
	48		21
	208		291
c	560	i	180
	56		15
	616		195
d	210	j	360
	42		27
	252		387
e	300	k	280
	30		16
	330		296
f	540	l	320
	18		72
	558		392

Task 2
a	135	d	576
b	336	e	234
c	140	f	392

Task 3
a	£78	e	£234
b	£360	f	£576
c	£315	g	£405
d	£392	h	£588

Sorcerer's Skill Check

E	V	I	F	Y	T	R	O	F
N	I	N	E	T	Y	S	I	X
I	D	G	W	U	L	Z	Y	Y
N	Y	T	H	G	I	E	T	T
Y	F	I	F	T	Y	P	E	R
T	S	I	X	T	Y	B	N	O
X	J	K	Z	N	M	O	I	F
I	F	I	F	T	Y	O	N	E
S	E	V	E	N	T	Y	C	E

a	60	g	50
b	81	h	45
c	90	i	40
d	96	j	51
e	80	k	70
f	69		

Pages 12–13

Task 1
a	1389	c	6768
b	5034	d	4858

Task 2
a	1735	c	2312
b	7400		

Task 3
a	4890	c	1980
b	2192	d	7011

Sorcerer's Skill Check
a	4560	c	2863
b	4810	d	3344

Pages 14–15

Challenge 1

Across		**Down**	
a	21	b	14
c	12	d	24
e	36	f	60
h	40	g	32
i	45	j	50
k	27	l	70
m	16	m	18
o	9	n	24
p	25		

Challenge 2
a 42   i 36
b 54   j 28
c 56   k 40
d 49   l 35
e 72   m 28
f 64   n 18
g 81   o 63
h 48   p 36

Challenge 3
a 8, 16, 32, 64, 128, 256, 512, 1024
b 28, 56, 112, 224, 448, 896, 1792, 3584
c 180, 360, 720, 1440, 2880, 5760, 11 520, 23 040

Challenge 4
a 9000   27 000   15 000
   24 000   72 000   40 000
   18 000   54 000   30 000
b 2000   4000   7000
   14 000   28 000   49 000
   16 000   32 000   56 000

Challenge 5
a £126   c £264
b £135   d £585

Challenge 6
a 1256   c 1770
b 5024   d 6975

Pages 16–17
Task 1 a $6 \times 2 = 12$ $12 \div 6 = 2$
     $2 \times 6 = 12$ $12 \div 2 = 6$
   b $7 \times 3 = 21$ $21 \div 7 = 3$
     $3 \times 7 = 21$ $21 \div 3 = 7$
   c $9 \times 2 = 18$ $18 \div 9 = 2$
     $2 \times 9 = 18$ $18 \div 2 = 9$
   d $4 \times 5 = 20$ $20 \div 4 = 5$
     $5 \times 4 = 20$ $20 \div 5 = 4$
   e $10 \times 3 = 30$ $30 \div 10 = 3$
     $3 \times 10 = 30$ $30 \div 3 = 10$
   f $4 \times 8 = 32$ $32 \div 4 = 8$
     $8 \times 4 = 32$ $32 \div 8 = 4$

Task 2 a 2   i 9
b 4   j 10
c 7   k 6
d 9   l 9
e 6   m 2
f 7   n 8
g 4   o 2
h 3   p 6

Sorcerer's Skill Check
a whale   c salt
b seal   d eel
Salt is the odd one out – all the others are creatures.

Pages 18–19
Task 1 a 5   g 6
b 2   h 3
c 9   i 8
d 4   j 3
e 10   k 7
f 2   l 7

Task 2 a 7   g 9
b 6   h 6
c 8   i 7
d 3   j 9
e 5   k 4
f 9   l 5

Task 3 a 8   d 6
b 3   e 7
c 5   f 2

Task 4 a 4   d 8
b 7p   e 5
c 9 cm

Sorcerer's Skill Check
a 35   f 8
b 4   g 12
c 3   h 4
d 9   i 7
e 80

Pages 20–21
Task 1 a 24   e 28
b 31   f 250
c 45   g 150
d 36   h 60

Task 2 a 54   e 148
b 115   f 157
c 84   g 371
d 225   h 168

Task 3 a 500   d 4200
b 1200   e 3800
c 2600   f 1800

Task 4 a £14   d £58
b £16   e £88
c £7.50   f £124.50

Sorcerer's Skill Check
a 200   100   50   25
b 1400   700   350   175
c 192   96   48   24   12   6
d 320   160   80   40   20   10

Pages 22–23
Task 1 a 710   e 100
b 120   f 550
c 300   g 80
d 970   h 26

Task 2 a 24   e 76
b 63   f 99
c 40   g 10
d 7   h 3

Task 3 $600 \div 100 \rightarrow 6$
    $1600 \div 10 \rightarrow 160$
    $9600 \div 100 \rightarrow 96$
    $3200 \div 10 \rightarrow 320$
    $320 \div 10 \rightarrow 32$
    $200 \div 10 \rightarrow 20$
    $600 \div 10 \rightarrow 60$
    $3200 \div 100 \rightarrow 32$

Sorcerer's Skill Check
a 570   g 14
b 190   h 7000
c 600   i 3
d 1100   j 6500
e 80   k 40
f 4000   l 900

Pages 24–25
Task 1 a 9 r 1   d 11 r 2
b 4 r 3   e 7 r 3
c 7 r 3   f 9 r 4

Task 2 a 17.5   e 4.2
b 6.25   f 8.5
c 7.5   g 10.75
d 3.2   h 5.5

Task 3 a £1.50   e £2.40
b 60p   f £1.75
c 80p   g £1.50
d £1.25   h £3.20

Sorcerer's Skill Check
a 2   d 1
b 5   e 7
c 3   f 1

Pages 26–27
Task 1 a 32 r 6   f 87 r 1
b 78 r 1   g 81 r 7
c 72 r 4   h 86 r 3
d 29 r 2   i 45 r 1
e 85 r 4   j 74 r 2

Task 2 a 3   d 8
b 3   e 6
c 9   f 6

Sorcerer's Skill Check
a 68 r 3   d 52 r 6
b 52 r 2   e 53 r 3
c 37 r 2

Pages 28–29
Challenge 1
a 9p   e 6
b 8   f 10
c 7   g 6 kg
d 3

Challenge 2
a 4   f 5
b 5   g 2
c 8   h 6
d 10   i 8
e 3

Challenge 3
a £7   d £17
b £13   e £24
c £25   f £31

Challenge 4
a 30   f 6
b 6700   g 800
c 850   h 72
d 320   i 5900
e 4   j 1

Challenge 5
a 6 r 1, 6.5   f 4 r 2, 4.25
b 7 r 4, 7.5   g 21 r 1, 21.5
c 5 r 1, 5.25   h 3 r 4, 3.8
d 6 r 3, 6.5   i 10 r 2, 10.4
e 2 r 3, 2.5

Challenge 6
a 234 r 1   c 56 r 7
b 61 r 1   d 173 r 1

Wizard's Certificate of Excellence

★ **Terrific Times Tables**

★ **Devilish Division Facts**

★ **Tricky Times Tables**

★ **Dastardly Division**

★ **Dazzling Doubling**

★ **Hazardous Halving**

★ **Marvellous Multiples**

★ **Dreamy Dividing**

★ **Magical Mental Methods**

★ **Revolting Remainders**

★ **Wacky Written Methods**

★ **Written Wizardry**

★ **Apprentice Wizard Challenge 1**

★ **Apprentice Wizard Challenge 2**

This is to state that Wizard Whimstaff awards

Apprentice _____

the title of Maths Wizard. Congratulations!

Wizard Whimstaff

Published 2002
10 9 8 7 6 5 4 3

Letts Educational, The Chiswick Centre,
414 Chiswick High Road, London W4 5TF
Tel 020 8996 3333   Fax 020 8742 8390
Email mail@lettsed.co.uk
www.letts-education.com

Text, design and illustrations © Letts Educational Ltd 2002

Author: Paul Broadbent
Book Concept and Development:
Helen Jacobs, Publishing Director; Sophie London, Project Editor
Design and Editorial: Cambridge Publishing Management Ltd.
Illustrations: Mike Phillips and Neil Chapman (Beehive Illustration)
Cover Illustration: Neil Chapman
Cover Design: Linda Males

Letts Educational Limited is a division of Granada Learning Limited.
Part of Granada plc.

British Library Cataloguing in Publication Data

A CIP record for this book is available from the British Library.

ISBN 1 84315 100 6

Printed in Italy

Colour reproduction by PDQ Digital Media Solutions Ltd, Bungay, Suffolk